FALL

SEASONS OF THE YEAR

by
Harriet Brundle

WINDMILL BOOKS
New York

SEASONS OF THE YEAR

Published in 2018 by **Windmill Books**, an Imprint of Rosen Publishing
29 East 21st Street, New York, NY 10010

Written by: Harriet Brundle
Edited by: Gemma McMullen
Designed by: Ian McMullen

Photo credits: Abbreviations: l-left, r-right, b-bottom, t-top, c-center, m-middle. All images are courtesy of Shutterstock.com.
Front Cover – Inara Prusakova. 1 – jordache. 3, 22l – Nagy-Bagoly Arpad. 4l Konstanttin. 4lc – djgis. 2, 4rc – Smileus. 4r – Triff. 5,
24 – Poznyakov. 6 – JonesHon. 7 – Liderina. 8 – Goran Bogicevic. 9 – Subbotina Anna. 10 – TessarTheTegu. 11 – ehtesham. 12 –
Soyka. 12inset – MNStudio. 13 – Catalin Petolea. 13 inset – Africa Studio. 14 – XiXinXing. 15l – stockphoto mania. 15r – gillmar. 16
– RonGreer.Com. 16 inset – Christian Jung. 17 – greenland. 18 – Samuel Borges Photography. 19 – Dasha Petrenko. 20 – etorres.
21 – Romrodphoto. 21 inset – Lesya Dolyuk. 22– BonD80. 23 – LilKar. 23 inset – S.Borisov.

Cataloging-in-Publication Data

Names: Brundle, Harriet.
Title: Fall / Harriet Brundle.
Description: New York : Windmill Books, 2018. | Series: Seasons of the year | Includes index.
Identifiers: ISBN 9781499484137 (pbk.) | ISBN 9781499484014 (library bound) | ISBN 9781499483932 (6 pack)
Subjects: LCSH: Autumn--Juvenile literature. | Seasons--Juvenile literature.
Classification: LCC QB637.7 B78 2017 | DDC 508.2--dc23

Manufactured in China

CPSIA Compliance Information: Batch #BS17WM: For Further Information contact
Rosen Publishing, New York, New York at 1-800-237-9932

Contents

4   Seasons of the Year

6   Fall

8   The Weather

10   Animals

12   Plants

14   In the Backyard

16   Food

18   What Do We Wear in the Fall?

20   Things to Do in the Fall

22   Fall Fun

24   Glossary & Index

Words that appear in **bold** can be found in the glossary on page 24.

Seasons of the Year

There are four seasons in a year. The seasons are called spring, summer, fall, and winter.

4

Every season is different.
This book is about fall!

Fall

Fall happens after summer and before winter. The fall months are September, October, November, and December.

January						
Sun	Mon	Tue	Wed	Thu	Fri	Sat
	2	3	4	5	6	7
	9	10	11	12	13	14
	16	17	18	19	20	21
	23	24	25	26	27	28
	30	31				

February						
Sun	Mon	Tue	Wed	Thu	Fri	Sat
			1	2	3	4
	6	7	8	9	10	11
	13	14	15	16	17	18
	20	21	22	23	24	25
	27	28	29			

March						
Sun	Mon	Tue	Wed	Thu	Fri	Sat
				1	2	3
4	5	6	7	8	9	10
11	12	13	14	15	16	17
18	19	20	21	22	23	24
25	26	27	28	29	30	31

April						
Sun	Mon	Tue	Wed	Thu	Fri	Sat
1	2	3	4	5	6	7
8	9	10	11	12	13	14
15	16	17	18	19	20	21
22	23	24	25	26	27	28
29	30					

May						
Sun	Mon	Tue	Wed	Thu	Fri	Sat
		1	2	3	4	5
7	8	9	10	11	12	
14	15	16	17	18	19	
21	22	23	24	25	26	
28	29	30	31			

June						
Sun	Mon	Tue	Wed	Thu	Fri	Sat
					1	2
4	5	6	7	8	9	
11	12	13	14	15	16	
18	19	20	21	22	23	
25	26	27	28	29	30	

July						
Sun	Mon	Tue	Wed	Thu	Fri	Sat
	2	3	4	5	6	7
	9	10	11	12	13	14
	16	17	18	19	20	21
	23	24	25	26	27	28
	30	31				

August						
Sun	Mon	Tue	Wed	Thu	Fri	Sat
			1	2	3	4
6	7	8	9	10	11	
13	14	15	16	17	18	
20	21	22	23	24	25	
27	28	29	30	31		

September						
Sun	Mon	Tue	Wed	Thu	Fri	Sat
						1
3	4	5	6	7	8	
10	11	12	13	14	15	
17	18	19	20	21	22	
24	25	26	27	28	29	

October						
Sun	Mon	Tue	Wed	Thu	Fri	Sat
	1	2	3	4	5	6
7	8	9	10	11	12	13
14	15	16	17	18	19	20
21	22	23	24	25	26	27
28	29	30	31			

November						
Sun	Mon	Tue	Wed	Thu	Fri	Sat
				1	2	3
4	5	6	7	8	9	10
11	12	13	14	15	16	17
18	19	20	21	22	23	24
25	26	27	28	29	30	

December						
Sun	Mon	Tue	Wed	Thu	Fri	Sat
						1
3	4	5	6	7	8	
10	11	12	13	14	15	
17	18	19	20	21	22	
24	25	26	27	28	29	
31						

The daytime feels shorter in the fall than in summer. This is because there are less hours of sunlight.

The Weather

The weather starts to get colder in the fall. There is often rain and wind.

It can be **foggy** in the fall. The fog makes it hard for us to see.

Animals

Animals must eat lots in the fall to prepare for the cold winter.

Animals need fat on their bodies to keep warm.

Spider

Web

On a cold fall morning, look out for spiders in their webs.

11

Plants

There are lots of berries on the bushes in the fall.

Be careful! Not all berries are safe for us to eat.

Pears grow in the fall.
They are a yummy treat.

Pear

In the Backyard

The leaves on the trees turn brown and red. They fall from the trees onto the ground.

Summer

Fall

As the weather gets colder, the summer plants start to die and the backyard changes color.

15

Food

Pumpkin

Pumpkins grow in the fall. We can use them to make pumpkin soup.

Which of these have you seen before?

Carrots

Beets

Root vegetables are ready to be eaten in the fall.

What Do We Wear in the Fall?

We may need our coats in the fall so we can stay warm if the weather is cold.

Coat

Don't forget your boots if it is raining!

Rain boots keep our feet from getting wet.

Things to Do in the Fall

In the fall, we celebrate Thanksgiving. We visit our family and are thankful for good things.

It is fun to pick the last of the apples left on the trees in the fall.

We can use them to make apple pie!

Fall Fun

Look at the leaves on the trees and on the ground. How many different colors can you see?

22

Did you know?
**The fall season
is also called
autumn.**

23

Glossary

Foggy: when a thick cloud of water hangs in the air making it hard for us to see.

Root Vegetables: types of vegetables that grow under the ground.

Thankful: feeling or showing thanks.

Index

Cold 8, 10, 11, 15, 18

Leaves 14, 22

Season 4, 5, 23

Summer 4, 6, 7, 15

Winter 4, 6, 10

24